ON LOVE AND BARLEY

BASHO, the Japanese poet and diarist, was born in Iga-ueno near Kyoto in 1644. He spent his youth as companion to the son of the local lord, and with him he studied the writing of seventeen-syllable verse. In 1667 he moved to Edo (now Tokyo) where he continued to write verse. He eventually became a recluse, living on the outskirts of Edo in a hut. When he travelled he relied entirely on the hospitality of temples and fellow-poets. In his writings he was strongly influenced by the Zen sect of Buddhism.

LUCIEN STRYK'S most recent collections of poetry are *Where We Are: Selected Poems and Zen Translations* (1997) and *And Still Birds Sing: New and Collected Poems* (1998). He has brought out two spoken albums of his poems on Folkways Records, a book of essays, *The Awakened Self: Encounters with Zen*, and, among other translations, *The Dumpling Field: Haiku of Issa* and *Cage of Fireflies: Modern Japanese Haiku. Zen, Poetry, the Art of Lucien Stryk* (edited by Susan Porterfield) appeared in 1993. He is editor of *World of the Buddha: An Introduction to Buddhist Literature* and the anthologies *Heartland: Poets of the Midwest* (I and II). With the late Takashi Ikemoto he translated *The Penguin Book of Zen Poetry, Zen Poems of China and Japan: The Crane's Bill* and *Triumph of the Sparrow: Zen Poems of Shinkichi Takahashi*. He has received fellowships from the National Endowment for the Arts, and the National Translation Center, and the Ford and Rockefeller foundations. He has held a Fulbright travel/research grant and two visiting lectureships in Japan.

On Love
and Barley:
Haiku
of Basho

Translated from
the Japanese
with an Introduction by
Lucien Stryk

Penguin Books

PENGUIN BOOKS

Published by the Penguin Group
Penguin Books Ltd, 80 Strand, London WC2R 0RL, England
Penguin Putnam Inc., 375 Hudson Street, New York, New York 10014, USA
Penguin Books Australia Ltd, 250 Camberwell Road, Camberwell, Victoria 3124, Australia
Penguin Books Canada Ltd, 10 Alcorn Avenue, Toronto, Ontario, Canada M4V 3B2
Penguin Books India (P) Ltd, 11 Community Centre, Panchsheel Park, New Delhi – 110 017, India
Penguin Books (NZ) Ltd, Cnr Rosedale and Airborne Roads, Albany, Auckland, New Zealand
Penguin Books (South Africa) (Pty) Ltd, 24 Sturdee Avenue, Rosebank 2196, South Africa

Penguin Books Ltd, Registered Offices: 80 Strand, London WC2R 0RL, England

www.penguin.com

First published 1985

047

Copyright © Lucien Stryk, 1985
All rights reserved

The illustrations are from an album of paintings by Taiga, reproduced
by kind permission of the Trustees of the British Museum

Printed and bound in Great Britain by Clays Ltd, Elcograf S.p.A.
Set in 10/14 pt Photina

ISBN-13: 978–0–140–44459–9

www.greenpenguin.co.uk

To Hiroshi Takaoka
with affection

Contents

Introduction

It is night: imagine, if you will, a path leading to a hut lost in a
wildly growing arbour, shaded by the *basho*, a wide-leafed banana
tree rare to Japan. A sliding door opens: an eager-eyed man in
monk's robe steps out, surveys his shadowy thicket and the purple
outline of a distant mountain, bends his head to catch the rush of
river just beyond; then, looking up at the sky, pauses a while, and
claps his hands. Three hundred years pass – the voice remains
fresh and exciting as that moment.

> Summer moon –
> clapping hands,
> I herald dawn.

So it was with Matsuo Kinsaku (1644–94), the first great haiku
poet, who would later change his name to Basho in honour of the
tree given him by a disciple.

Basho appeared on the scene soon after the so-called Dark Age
of Japanese literature (1425–1625), a time of the popularization
of purely indigenous verse forms, and the brilliant beginning of
the Tokugawa era (1603–1867). The haiku was already well
established, with its own distinct rules, but in the hands of rule-
smiths (as in the sonnet of Western verse) it was expiring of
artificiality. Almost alone, Basho reinvigorated the form. How he
did so is, fortunately, well known, for among his many admirers
were a few far-seeing enough to record his comments, literally to
catch him on the run, for he was always a compulsive traveller,
wandering all over Japan in search of new sights and experiences.

He wrote at least one thousand haiku, as well as a number of

travel sketches, which contain some of his finest poems. One of
the sketches, *The Records of a Travel-Worn Satchel*, begins with a
most revealing account of what poetry meant to him:

> In this poor body, composed of one hundred bones and nine openings,
> is something called spirit, a flimsy curtain swept this way and that by the
> slightest breeze. It is spirit, such as it is, which led me to poetry, at first
> little more than a pastime, then the full business of my life. There have
> been times when my spirit, so dejected, almost gave up the quest, other
> times when it was proud, triumphant. So it has been from the very start,
> never finding peace with itself, always doubting the worth of what it
> makes . . . All who achieve greatness in art – Saigyo in traditional poetry,
> Sogi in linked verse, Sesshu in painting, Rikyu in tea ceremony – possess
> one thing in common: they are one with nature.

Towards the end of his life Basho cautioned fellow haiku poets
to rid their minds of superficiality by means of what he called
karumi (lightness). This quality, so important to all arts linked to
Zen (Basho had become a monk), is the artistic expression of non-
attachment, the result of calm realization of profoundly felt truths.
Here, from a preface to one of his works, is how the poet pictures
karumi: 'In my view a good poem is one in which the form of the
verse, and the joining of its two parts, seem light as a shallow
river flowing over its sandy bed.'

Basho's mature haiku style, *Shofu*, is known not only for *karumi*,
but also for two other Zen-inspired aesthetic ideals: *sabi* and *wabi*.
Sabi implies contented solitariness, and in Zen is associated with
early monastic experience, when a high degree of detachment is
cultivated. *Wabi* can be described as the spirit of poverty, an
appreciation of the commonplace, and is perhaps most fully
achieved in the tea ceremony, which, from the simple utensils
used in the preparation of the tea to the very structure of the tea
hut, honours the humble.

Basho perceived, early in his career, that the first haiku writers,
among them Sokan (1458–1546) and Moritake (1472–1549),

while historically of much importance, had little to offer poets of his day. These early writers had created the haiku form by establishing the autonomy of the parts of *haikai renga*, sequences of seventeen-syllable verses composed by poets working together. Though their poems possessed the desired terseness, they did not adequately evoke nature and, for the most part, lacked *karumi*. Basho wove his poems so closely around this feeling of lightness that at times he dared ignore time-honoured elements of the form, including the syllabic limitation. The following piece, among his greatest, consists in the original of eighteen syllables:

> Kareeda ni
> Karasu no tomarikeri
> Aki no kure

> On the dead limb
> squats a crow –
> autumn night.

So rare in the history of haiku was such licence that three hundred years on, a new haiku school, the Soun, or free-verse, school, justified its abandonment of syllabic orthodoxy on the grounds that Japan's greatest poet had not been constrained by such rules. In most respects, however, Basho was a traditionalist, his poems following very closely the expected structural development: two elements divided by a break (*kireji*, or 'cutting word', best rendered in English by emphatic punctuation), the first element being the condition or situation – 'Spring air', in the first of the following examples – the other the sudden perception, preceded by *kireji* (in these pieces a dash).

> Spring air –
> woven moon
> and plum scent.

Early autumn –
rice field, ocean,
one green.

Unknown spring –
plum blossom
behind the mirror.

So the poet presents an observation of a natural, often commonplace event, in plainest diction, without verbal trickery. The effect is one of spareness, yet the reader is aware of a microcosm related to transcendent unity. A moment, crystallized, distilled, snatched from time's flow, and that is enough. All suggestion and implication, the haiku event is held precious because, in part, it demands the reader's participation: without a sensitive audience it would appear unimpressive. Haiku's great popularity is only partly due to its avoidance of the forbidding obscurities found in other kinds of verse: more important, it is likely to give the reader a glimpse of hitherto unrecognized depths in the self.

As we have seen, the sobriquet Basho, amusing even to his fellow countrymen, was taken by the poet from a tree planted by the hut in which he lived and met disciples, perhaps because it suggested the lightness he sought in life and art. He loved the name, making many references to it in writing. In Japan, too cold for the tree to bear fruit, the *basho* was thought exotic, and though its trunk had no practical use its big soft leaves offered fine shade in summer. Each of the three huts the poet was to own throughout his life was called the Basho hut, the tree transplanted wherever he settled. Even on his journeys he seemed never to be away from his hut, as the following poem suggests:

Banana leaves hanging
round my hut –
must be moon-viewing.

Little is known of the poet's early life. It is believed he was born in or near Ueno in Iga Province, around thirty miles south-east of Kyoto. He had an elder brother and four sisters. His father, Matsuo Yozaemon, possibly a low-ranking samurai, farmed in times of peace, making a modest yet respectable living. Of the poet's mother all we know is that it is unlikely that she was a native of Ueno. About the time of his father's death in 1656, Basho entered the service of the samurai Todo Yoshitada, a young relative of the local feudal lord. He was very well treated, and it was in these years that he began writing verse (his earliest known work is dated 1662). When Yoshitada died, prematurely, in 1666, the poet resigned his position and moved, it is thought, to Kyoto. A few of Basho's biographers mention a mistress (who was to become a nun named Jutei), even a child or two – but all concerning that part of his life is sheerest speculation.

It is known for certain that by 1672 Basho was in Edo (modern Tokyo), hoping for a literary career. He wrote, among other things, a pair of hundred-verse *renku* with another poet, critical commentaries for *Haiku Contests in Eighteen Rounds*, produced an anthology of his own and his best pupils' work, *Best Poems of Tosei's Twenty Disciples* (he was then called Tosei), and, like all haiku teachers then and since, judged one contest after another, including 'The Rustic Haiku Contest' and 'The Evergreen Haiku Contest'. Soon he settled in his first Basho hut, built for him in 1680 by an admirer, Sampu, in Fukagawa, in an isolated spot near the Sumida river, and it was here that he began to attract, not pupils, but disciples. From the start of his career as an established master he drew the most promising young Edo haiku poets, who came seeking advice and, on occasion, to engage with him in composition of linked verse. Later, there were periods when he found visitors no longer bearable, so he would keep his gate locked:

> Morning-glory trailing –
> all day the gate-
> bolt's fastened.

Basho loved and needed solitude: 'I am like a sick man weary of society,' he wrote. 'There was a time I wanted an official post, land of my own, another time I would have liked to live in a monastery. Yet I wandered on, a cloud in the wind, wanting only to capture the beauty of flowers and birds.' But from the start of his residence near Edo he engaged with disciples in profound discussion of the art of haiku, and was soon known as the foremost living theorist. Here, one of his disciples, Doho, writes of a conversation with the poet:

> The master said, 'Learn about a pine tree from a pine tree, and about a bamboo stalk from a bamboo stalk.' What he meant was that the poet should detach his mind from self . . . and enter into the object, sharing its delicate life and its feelings. Whereupon a poem forms itself. Description of the object is not enough: unless a poem contains feelings which have come from the object, the object and the poet's self will be separate things.

To give an indication of the influence of such comments on subsequent practice of the art, a contemporary haiku school, Tenro, possesses a creed, *Shasei* (on-the-spot composition, with the subject 'traced to its origin'), virtually based on the theoretical statements and practice of Basho. Tenro has some two thousand members all over Japan, and it is customary for groups to meet at a designated spot, perhaps a Zen temple in a place famous for its pines or bamboo, and there write as many as one hundred haiku in a day, attempting to enter the object, 'share its delicate life and feelings'. As might be expected, there is much imitation of the master. Yet Basho was severe with disciples who did little more than imitate him:

> Rhyming imitators –
> musk melons
> whacked to halves.

Basho's prose was as distinctive as his poetry, often taking the form of *haibun* (prose followed by haiku), characteristically concrete and imagistic. Writers of *haibun* used many Chinese characters (ideograms), which in contrast to phonetic Japanese have a strong visual effect. Thus the prose was consonant with the verse it accompanied. Perhaps Basho's finest prose, and most impressive haiku, can be found in the remarkable travel sketches he composed throughout his restless life, including *The Records of a Weather-Exposed Skeleton* (1684–5), *A Visit to Kashima Shrine* (1687), *The Records of a Travel-Worn Satchel* (1688) and, most ambitious of all, *The Narrow Road to the Deep North*, begun in 1689. In the best of these sketches, and always in the late ones, prose and verse work organically together, and though, following him, many have produced similar works in various forms and languages, his stand alone for their absolute naturalness.

It is especially in the travel sketches that the poet's profound debt to Zen is apparent. Like other haiku poets of his time Basho considered himself a Zennist, indeed was thought to be a Zen monk. It is known that he practised the discipline under the master Buccho, with whom, according to D. T. Suzuki in *The Essentials of Zen Buddhism* (1963), he had the following exchange:

Buccho: How are you getting along these days?
Basho: After a recent rain the moss has grown greener than ever.
Buccho: What Buddhism is there prior to the greenness of moss?
Basho: A frog jumps into the water, hear the sound!

It has been claimed that this exchange, inspiration for one of the poet's best-known poems, began an epoch in the history of haiku.

All his life a wanderer, Basho took full advantage of the safe-conduct – important to the traveller of his day – and mobility Zen priesthood offered. He gave up virtually all possessions, his only concern spiritual and artistic discovery.

> First winter rain –
> I plod on,
> Traveller, my name.

Basho's discussion of poetry was always tinged by Zen thought, and what in his maturity he advocated above all was the realization of *muga*, so close an identification with the things one writes of that self is forgotten. As Zen's Sixth Patriarch, Hui-neng (637–712), put it, one should not look at, but *as*, the object. It is of course one thing to voice ideals, another to attain them. Basho's late poems demonstrate that, in spite of periods of acute self-doubt, he was able to achieve a unity of life and art, the great hope of Zen creators. 'What is important,' he wrote, 'is to keep mind high in the world of true understanding, then, returning to daily experience, seek therein the true and the beautiful. No matter what the activity of the moment, we must never forget it has a bearing on everlasting self, our poetry.' As D. T. Suzuki explains, haiku has always been one with Zen:

When a feeling reaches its highest pitch, we remain silent, even 17 syllables may be too many. Japanese artists . . . influenced by the way of Zen tend to use the fewest words or strokes of brush to express their feelings. When they are too fully expressed no room for suggestion is possible, and suggestibility is the secret of the Japanese arts.

Though inspired by Zen, Basho's haiku avoided the didactic tone of much classical Zen poetry, even the greatest:

WAKA ON THE DIAMOND SUTRA

Coming, going, the waterfowl
Leaves not a trace,
Nor does it need a guide.

Firm on the seven Buddhas' cushion,
Centre, centre. Here's the arm-rest

My master handed down. Now, to it!
Head up, eyes straight, ears in line with shoulders.

WAKA ON ZEN SITTING

Scarecrow in the hillock
Paddy-field –
How unaware! How useful!

Written by Dogen (1200–1253), who in the Kamakura period introduced Soto Zen to Japan, such poems were meant to encourage disciples. Dogen did not think himself a poet: he was, like all Zen masters, a guide, whose mission was to point minds to enlightenment, and the poems he wrote were meant only to serve that end. Basho, on the other hand, was conscious of being an artist, and saw the conceptual, whatever its application, as the enemy of art.

Basho strove to place his reader within an experience whose unfolding might lead to revelation, the eternal wrested from the phenomenal world. As a mystic, he knew the unconditioned was attainable only within the conditioned, *nirvana* within *samsara* – that the illumination sought was to be found in the here and now of daily life. Throughout Zen's history, wherever practised, Zennists have perceived a process in all such matters, some relating it to doctrines such as the *Avatamsaka*, a Mahayana Buddhist *sutra* of great importance to the formation of Zen. Here, for example, is how the contemporary master Taigan Takayama interprets a poem by Japan's greatest living Zen poet, Shinkichi Takahashi. First, the poem:

THE PEACH

A little girl under a peach tree,
Whose blossoms fall into the entrails
Of the earth.

There you stand, but a mountain may be there
Instead; it is not unlikely that the earth
May be yourself.

You step against a plate of iron and half
Your face is turned to iron. I will smash
Flesh and bone

And suck the cracked peach. She went up the mountain
To hide her breasts in the snowy ravine.
Women's legs

Are more or less alike. The leaves of the peach tree
Stretch across the sea to the end of
The continent.

The sea was at the little girl's beck and call.
I will cross the sea like a hairy
Caterpillar

And catch the odour of your body.

Now, Taigan Takayama's comment:

Most interesting, from both the Zen and literary points of view. Let's begin with the former: an Avatamsaka doctrine holds that the universe can be observed from the four angles of (1) phenomena, (2) noumenon, (3) the identity of noumenon and phenomena, and (4) the mutual identity of phenomena. Now, whether he was aware of it or not, the poet depicted a world in which noumenon and phenomena are identical. Considering the poem with Zen in mind, the lesson to be drawn, I suppose, is that one should not loiter on the way but proceed straight to one's destination – the viewpoint of the mutual identity of phenomena. But from a literary point of view, the significance, and the charm, of the poem lies in its metaphorical presentation of a world in which noumenon and phenomena are identified with each other [*Zen: Poems, Prayers, Sermons, Anecdotes, Interviews*].

It is unlikely that Basho would have disagreed with Taigan

Takayama, yet there is little doubt he would also have claimed that haiku, at its best, depicts a world in which 'noumenon and phenomena are identical'. Indeed he might have insisted, with justice, that it exists to demonstrate such identity. Occasionally, to be sure, Basho wrote poems as explicit in their Zen intention as any master's:

> Skylark on moor –
> sweet song
> of non-attachment.

> Monks, morning-glories –
> how many under
> the pine-tree Law?

> Four temple gates –
> under one moon,
> four sects.

Yet surely the chief reason for the poet's universal appeal is that he never leaves nature, which – East, West – is one, through all processes and manifestations the sole unchanging thing we know. Throughout his life as a wanderer Basho sought to celebrate: whether his eyes turned to mountain or gorge, whether his ears heard thunder or bird-song, whether his foot brushed flower or mud, he was intensely alive to the preciousness of all that shared the world with him. Even his final poem, written for disciples shortly before his death, reaches for the unknown:

> Sick on a journey –
> over parched fields
> dreams wander on.

Acknowledgements

For permission to use material first printed by them, I owe thanks to the editors and publishers of *American Poetry Review*, *Asiaweek Literary Review*, *London Magazine*, *New Letters*, *Par Rapport*, *The Present Tense*, *Bird of Time* (The Flatlands Press, 1983) and *Traveller*, *My Name* (Embers Handpress, 1984).

Once again I find myself in debt to Takashi Ikemoto, co-translator of many years, who some time before his death in 1980 not only encouraged me to undertake this work of translation but gave me much valuable advice. I also owe much, once again, to the poet Shinkichi Takahashi, who pointed out for me the Zen in Basho's work. This collection has but one purpose, to suggest the spirit of Basho's haiku.

ON BASHO'S 'FROG'

Under the cloudy cliff, near the temple door,
Between dusky spring plants on the pond,
A frog jumps in the water, plop!
Startled, the poet drops his brush.

Sengai (1750–1837)

1

In my new robe
this morning –
someone else.

2

Fields, mountains
of Hubaku, in
nine days – spring.

3

Year by year,
the monkey's mask
reveals the monkey.

4

New Year – the Basho-Tosei
hermitage
a-buzz with haiku.

5

New Year –
feeling broody
from late autumn.

6

Spring come – New Year's
gourd stuffed, five quarts
of last year's rice.

7

Plunging hoofs stir
Futami sand – divine white
horse greets New Year.

8

Spring night,
cherry-
blossom dawn.

9

Wearing straw cloaks,
with spring
saints greet each other.

10

Spring's exodus –
birds shriek,
fish eyes blink tears.

11

Ploughing the field
for cherry-hemp –
storm echoes.

12

Spring rain –
under trees
a crystal stream.

13

Monks' feet clomping
through icy dark,
drawing sweet water.

14

Spring moon –
flower face
in mist.

15

Spring rain –
they rouse me,
old sluggard.

16

Ebb tide –
willows
dip to mud.

17

Sparrows in eaves,
mice in ceiling –
celestial music.

18

Dark night –
plover crying
for its nest.

19

Over skylark's song
Noh cry
of pheasant.

20

How terrible
the pheasant's call –
snake-eater.

21

Hozo mountain-pass
soars
higher than the skylark.

22

Bush-warbler dots
the rice-ball
drying on the porch.

23

Bucking the oven
gap – cat
yowls in heat.

24

Now cat's done
mewing, bedroom's
touched by moonlight.

25

Do not forget the plum,
blooming
in the thicket.

26

Spring air –
woven moon
and plum scent.

27

Mountain path –
sun rising
through plum scent.

28

Another haiku?
Yet more cherry blossoms –
not my face.

29

Sleeping willow –
soul of
the nightingale.

30

Behind the virgins'
quarters,
one blossoming plum.

31

First cherry
budding
by peach blossoms.

32

Red plum blossoms:
where behind the
bead-screen's love?

33

Pretending to drink
sake from my fan,
sprinkled with cherry petals.

34

If I'd the knack
I'd sing like
cherry flakes falling.

35

Striding ten, twelve
miles in search of
cherry wreaths – how glorious.

36

Under the cherry –
blossom soup,
blossom salad.

37

Reeling with *sake*
and cherry blossoms,
a sworded woman in *haori*.

38

Boozy on blossoms –
dark rice,
white *sake*.

39

Come out, bat –
birds, earth itself
hauled off by flowers.

40

Waterfall garlands –
tell
that to revellers.

41

Spraying in wind,
through blossoms,
waves of Lake Grebe.

42

Be careful where
you aim,
peaches of Fushimi.

43

Sparrows
in rape-field,
blossom-viewing.

44

Cold white azalea –
lone nun
under thatched roof.

45

Draining the *sake*
cask – behold,
a gallon flower-vase.

46

On my knees, hugging
roots, I grieve
for Priest Tando.

47

Taros sprouting
at the gate,
young creepers.

48

Search carefully –
in the hedge,
a shepherd's purse.

49

Aged – eating
laver, my teeth
grind sand.

50

Cherry blossoms –
lights
of years past.

51

Squalls shake the Basho
tree – all
night my basin echoes rain.

52

On the dead limb
squats a crow –
autumn night.

53

Kiyotaki river –
pine needles wildfire
on the crest.

54

Parting,
straw-clutching
for support.

55

Yellow rose petals
thunder –
a waterfall.

56

Whiter than stones
of Stone Mountain –
autumn wind.

57

Sparrow, spare
the horsefly
dallying in flowers.

58

Drizzly June –
long hair, face
sickly white.

59

Nara's Buddhas,
one by one –
essence of asters.

60

Darkening waves –
cry of wild ducks,
faintly white.

61

Faceless – bones
scattered in the field,
wind cuts my flesh.

62

Where cuckoo
vanishes –
an island.

63

Winter downpour –
even the monkey
needs a raincoat.

64

June clouds,
at ease on
Arashiyama peak.

65

Butterfly –
wings curve into
white poppy.

66

Summer wraps –
is there no end
to lice?

67

First winter rain –
I plod on,
Traveller, my name.

68

How quiet –
locust-shrill
pierces rock.

69

Wild mallow fringing
the wood,
plucked by my horse.

70

Futami friends, farewell –
clam torn from shell,
I follow autumn.

71

Traveller sleeps –
a sick wild duck reels
through cold night.

72

When I bend low
enough, purseweed
beneath my fence.

73

Poet grieving over shivering
monkeys, what of this child
cast out in autumn wind?

74

Poor boy – leaves
moon-viewing
for rice-grinding.

75

Wake, butterfly –
it's late, we've miles
to go together.

76

Violets –
how precious on
a mountain path.

77

Gulping June
rains, swollen
Mogami river.

78

Early autumn –
rice field, ocean,
one green.

79

Bright moon: I
stroll around the pond –
hey, dawn has come.

80

Storming over
Lake Nio, whirlwinds
of cherry blossoms.

81

From moon-wreathed
bamboo grove,
cuckoo song.

82

Visiting tombs,
white-hairs bow
over canes.

83

Skylark on moor –
sweet song
of non-attachment.

84

Clouds –
a chance to dodge
moon-viewing.

85

Autumn storm –
wild boars tossed
with leaves.

86

Waves scaling
Sado Island –
heaven's stream.

87

Between Suma's waves,
bush-clover
sparkled with shells.

88

Cuckoo –
sing, fly, sing,
then start again.

89

Moon-daubed bush-clover –
ssh, in the next room
snoring prostitutes.

90

Bird of time –
in Kyoto, pining
for Kyoto.

91

To lie drunk
on cobbles,
bedded in pinks.

92

Ise's shrine –
what tree can give
such perfume?

93

Peony –
the bee can't bear
to part.

94

Has it returned,
the snow
we viewed together?

95

No moon, no flowers,
no friend –
and he drinks *sake*.

96

Unknown spring –
plum blossom
behind the mirror.

97

Autumn's end –
how does my
neighbour live?

98

Village of no bells –
spring evenings,
what's to listen for?

99

Old legs, still eager
for Yoshino's
flowering slopes.

100

Octopus traps –
summer's moonspun dreams,
soon ended.

101

Autumn winds –
look, the chestnut
never more green.

102

Flower under harvest
sun – stranger
to bird, butterfly.

103

No rice in the
gourd? Then try
a maiden flower.

104

No hat, and cold
rain falling –
well!

105

Lightning –
heron-cry
stabs darkness.

106

Fading bells –
now musky blossoms
peal in dusk.

107

Sudden sun upon
the mountain path,
plum scent.

108

Though bush-clover
always stirs,
not one dewdrop falls.

109

Mogami river, yanking
the burning sky
into the sea.

110

Cicada – did it
chirp till it
knew nothing else?

111

Rain-washed
camellia – as it
falls, showers.

112

Spring – through
morning mist,
what mountain's there?

113

Noon doze,
wall cool against
my feet.

114

Beyond waves,
reaching far, the
cuckoo's song.

115

Smell of autumn –
heart longs for
the four-mat room.

116

Temple bell,
a cloud of cherry flowers –
Ueno? Asakusa?

117

To the willow –
all hatred, and desire
of your heart.

118

Nothing more lonely –
heart-shaped
paulownia leaf.

119

'Now darkness falls,'
quail chirps,
'what use hawk-eyes?'

120

Atop the mushroom –
who knows from where –
a leaf!

121

Birth of art –
song of rice planters,
chorus from nowhere.

122

Cresting Lake Omi's
seven misted views,
Miidera's bells.

123

Over Benkei's temple,
flashing Yoshitune's
sword – May carp.

124

Cormorant fishing:
how stirring,
how saddening.

125

Skylark sings all
day, and day
not long enough.

126

Year's end –
still in straw hat
and sandals.

127

Moonlit plum tree –
wait,
spring will come.

128

Snowy morning –
one crow
after another.

129

Come, see real
flowers
of this painful world.

130

Morning-glory –
it, too,
turns from me.

131

Travel-weary,
I seek lodging –
ah, wistaria.

132

Come, let's go
snow-viewing
till we're buried.

133

Chrysanthemum
silence – monk
sips his morning tea.

134

Crow's
abandoned nest,
a plum tree.

135

Melon
in morning dew,
mud-fresh.

136

Wintry day,
on my horse
a frozen shadow.

137

Summer moon –
clapping hands,
I herald dawn.

138

Drenched bush-clover,
passers-by –
both beautiful.

139

Harsh sound –
hail spattering
my traveller's hat.

140

Lips too chilled
for prattle –
autumn wind.

141

Not one traveller
braves this road –
autumn night.

142

Withered grass,
under piling
heat-waves.

143

Phew –
dace-guts scent
waterweed.

144

June rain,
hollyhocks turning
where sun should be.

145

Journey's end –
still alive, this
autumn evening.

146

How cold –
leek tips
washed white.

147

Firefly-viewing –
drunken steersman,
drunken boat.

148

Dewy shoulders
of my paper robe –
heat-waves.

149

Rainy days –
silkworms droop
on mulberries.

150

Still breathing
in an icy lump –
sea slugs.

151

Autumn moon,
tide foams to
the very gate.

152

Girl cat, so
thin on love
and barley.

153

Old pond,
leap-splash –
a frog.

154

Waterjar cracks –
I lie awake
this icy night.

155

Awaiting snow,
poets in their cups
see lightning flash.

156

Shrieking plovers,
calling darkness
around Hoshizaki Cape.

157

To the capital –
snow-clouds forming,
half the sky to go.

158

Dozing on horseback,
smoke from tea-fires
drifts to the moon.

159

Buddha's death-day –
old hands
clicking rosaries.

160

Year's end, all
corners of this
floating world, swept.

161

Autumn – even
birds and clouds
look old.

162

Cedar umbrella, off
to Mount Yoshino for
the cherry blossoms.

點綴數式

163

May rain – the thing
revealed, bridge
over Seta Bay.

164

Moor: point
my horse
where birds sing.

165

Autumn wind,
blasting the stones
of Mount Asama.

166

Orchid – breathing
incense into
butterfly's wings.

167

Dusk – though last
bell's faded,
air's cherry-rich.

168

Loneliness –
caged cricket dangling
from the wall.

169

High wind – tea
leaves whip against
the brushwood gate.

170

Rhyming imitators –
musk melons
whacked to halves.

171

By the azalea
crock, she strips
dried codfish.

172

Dawn-scaling –
a whitefish, with an
inch of whiteness.

173

Perfect moon –
this bole of tree
I've axed.

174

Month's end – no
moon, storm stripping
thousand-year cedars.

175

Insect song – over
winter's garden
moon's hair-thin.

176

Parched grass –
heat-waves shimmer,
one, two inches high.

177

Clear night, sound
of cloth-pounding
hails the Big Dipper.

178

Spider, are you
crying – or
the autumn wind?

179

Dipping moon,
sea-pungent
rice wine.

180

Slicing winter
gusts – rocks
among cedars.

181

Morning-glory trailing –
all day the gate-
bolt's fastened.

182

Pommelling hail –
like the old oak,
I never change.

183

Voices piercing
by the sliding door –
autumn wind.

184

Edo relic –
Fuji wind calm
on the fan.

185

Mirroring each other:
white narcissi,
paper screen.

186

Sound of rapids –
silent yellow petals
of the mountain rose.

187

Cuckoo –
moonlight binds
the thick bamboo.

188

Thousand isles greening
the summer sea –
Matsushima.

189

However close I look,
not a speck on
white chrysanthemum.

190

Autumn eve – please
turn to me. I,
too, am stranger.

191

Monks, morning-glories –
how many under
the pine-tree Law?

192

Taro leaves – beyond
the village a poor
farmer waits the moon.

193

Such fragrance –
from where,
which tree?

194

How sad – under
the battered helmet,
cricket song.

195

Man's end –
a bamboo shoot,
or less.

196

Husking rice,
a child squints up
to view the moon.

197

Snow-whisk sweeping
this path,
forgets the snow.

198

Walk boldly on,
through fly-swarms
into Kiso.

199

How I long to see
among dawn flowers,
the face of God.

200

Squid-seller,
harping cuckoo –
one voice.

201

Summer grove –
pasania tree and I
find shelter.

202

A weathered
skeleton –
how cold the wind.

203

Winter retreat –
how old the pine traced
on the golden screen.

204

While moon sets
atop the trees,
leaves cling to rain.

205

Sixteen-foot Buddha –
from your stone base,
rising heat-waves.

206

Travelling Kiso road,
through the heart
of pasania blooms.

207

Banana leaves hanging
round my hut –
must be moon-viewing.

208

Chestnuts of Kiso –
mementoes for
the floating world.

209

Coldest days –
dried salmon,
gaunt pilgrim.

210

Summer rain –
on the hut-wall traces
of poem-cards.

211

Samurai talk –
tang
of horse-radish.

212

Guest's shadow through
the paper screen – I sit dreaming
over charcoal fumes.

213

Oars slap waves –
this mournful night,
guts freeze.

214

You'd hear the
bagworm's song?
Come to my hut.

215

You the butterfly –
I, Chuang Tzu's
dreaming heart.

216

Year-end sprucing,
carpenter
hanging his *own* shelf.

217

Whitebait – black
eyes haul in
the net of Law.

218

Light the fire –
how about this,
a giant snowball.

219

Friends part
forever – wild geese
lost in cloud.

220

How pleasant –
just once *not* to see
Fuji through mist.

221

Muddy *sake*, black rice –
sick of the cherry,
sick of the world.

222

Crescent moon lights
buckwheat flowers –
this hazy earth.

223

In the garden
a sweaty shoe – scent
of chrysanthemum.

224

Cuckoo's cry,
bouncing
on lake-waves.

225

Rock azaleas,
flushed red
by cuckoo's cry.

226

Hail beats on
the new house – old
self's a mossy oak.

227

Grey flower-guards,
heads together,
gab under the cherry.

228

Dying cricket –
how full of
life, his song.

229

Here, to repay your
kindness – leaves
of garden willow.

230

Irises blooming
from my feet –
sandals laced in blue.

231

Old fan scribbled
with poems –
shredded by summer's end.

232

House of fancy –
dozing there, it
was all mine.

233

Small hut in
summer grove, untouched
by woodpeckers.

234

Shower of white
plum blossoms –
where are the cranes?

235

What stroke of luck –
hawk spied above
Irago promontory.

236

Four temple gates –
under one moon,
four sects.

237

Cool beach of Fukuura –
at my back
sun-fired Mount Atsumi.

238

When the girls planted
the last rice-seed,
I stepped from willow's shade.

239

One of the joys
of travel – rare
talk about an iris.

240

Beyond potato fields,
temple gate
lost in goose-grass.

241

Fish shop –
how cold the lips
of salted bream.

242

Mad with poetry,
I stride like Chikusai
into the wind.

243

Gorge-spanning bridge,
ivy braiding
body, spirit – one.

244

Not a flaw on
the divine glass,
drenched with snow-flowers.

245

South Valley –
wind brings
a scent of snow.

246

From the heart
of the sweet peony,
a drunken bee.

247

Cow carting fern and rice-
cakes, this year of the
cow – whose bride are you?

248

Town merchants,
who will buy this hat
lacquered with snow?

249

Together let's eat
ears of wheat,
share a grass pillow.

250

Dew-drops –
how better wash away
world's dust?

251

Tomb, bend
to autumn wind –
my sobbing.

252

Summer grasses,
all that remains
of soldiers' dreams.

253

Sick on a journey –
over parched fields
dreams wander on.

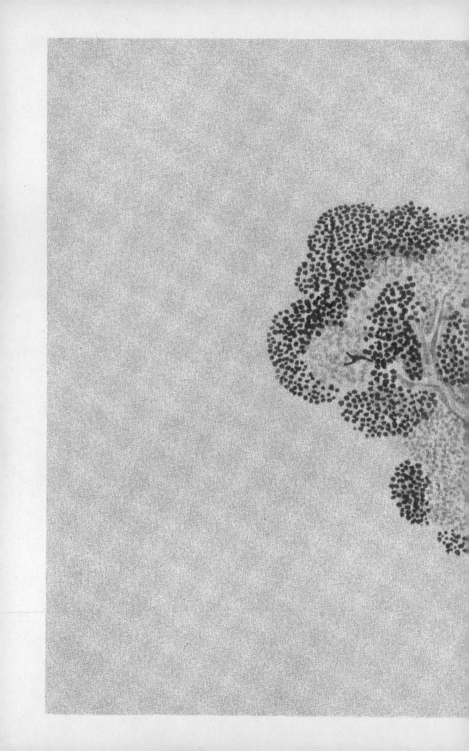

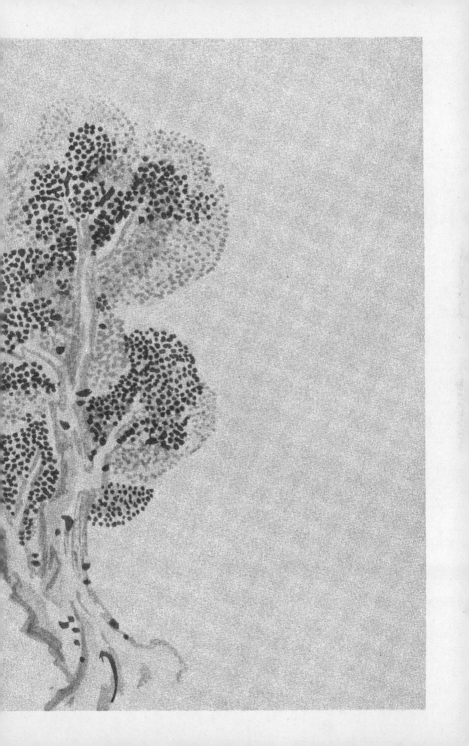

Notes

2

Hubaku was a district near Kyoto known for its orchards. Nine days: not even a ten-day period, a conventional Japanese time-division.

3

In Japanese literature the monkey is often used to satirize human foibles.

4

Basho, whose first pseudonym was Tosei, lived in the Basho-Tosei hermitage (hut) from 1680 to 1692.

6

Gourds were used as rice containers.

7

Shinto worshippers at Ise Shrine still purify themselves in the tide of Futami beach before praying to the rising sun of the New Year.

9

Basho's ideal, like poet-priest Saigyo's, was the beggar-saints who roamed the roads in spring.

11

Hemp was planted during the cherry season, not in winter.

12

This is a reference to the 'crystal' stream near poet-priest Saigyo's hermitage.

13

One by one, on the anniversary of the Buddha's death in mid
February, monks of Nigatsudo (February Hall) in Nara draw sweet
water from the temple well.

18

The plover builds its nest in the sand by the shore, thus can easily
lose it.

19

Like the grief-cries of actors in *Noh* theatre, the pheasant's call is
thought pathetic.

21

Hozo mountain-pass is near Kyoto, between Atagoyama and
Arashiyama mountains.

22

Rice-balls, a delicacy served on special occasions and always at
New Year, are dried in the sun.

25

A 'parting' haiku meant for a disciple about to leave on a journey.
The 'plum' is Basho himself.

30

Virgins (*okorago*) served in the Shinto rituals at Ise Shrine.

32

The suggestion here is that behind a bead-screen one is tempted
by love.

33

In *Noh* theatre actors pretend to drink *sake* from fans, tipped up
like cups.

35

In the original, five, six *ri*: one *ri* is equal to about two and a half miles.

36

Today, as in Basho's day, picnics are held under the trees in cherry-blossom time.

37

Women would not have worn a *haori* (half-coat), nor carried a sword.

38

Dark rice and white *sake* suggest poverty.

39

The bat symbolizes a priest.

41

Lake Grebe is Lake Biwa, near Kyoto, known for its grebes.

42

Fushimi peaches are very large, thus risky to walk under.

45

Gallon: in the original two *sho*. One *sho* is equal to about half a gallon. Old *sake* containers are still prized, often as much as vases.

46

Nothing is known of the poet's friend, Priest Tando.

47

The *taro* is an edible tropical plant which, to the Japanese, has the taste of haiku.

53

The Kiyotaki river flows near Kyoto.

54

Another parting poem, meant for disciples Basho was about to leave.

56

The poet is using a metaphor: it is not known to which mountain he is here referring.

59

Nara, established as Japan's first permanent capital in 710 by Empress-Regnant Gemmyo, was the cradle of its arts and crafts and the centre of Buddhism. It still has many great Buddhist temples and relics.

64

The Arashiyama district, near Kyoto and dominated by the mountain of that name, is thought to be one of Japan's most beautiful.

70

Basho had been visiting Ise Shrine and friends at nearby Futami – hence the beach imagery.

74

In the poet's day children worked in the fields alongside adults.

77

The Mogami river has powerful rapids at a point between Furukuchi and Kiyokawa.

80

Lake Nio, famous for cherry trees along its shores.

82

On the first day of the Bon Festival (13–15 July) it is customary for Buddhists to visit family tombs and symbolically invite the dead to return to their homes.

83

As a Zennist, Basho was aware of the need to realize the state of non-attachment.

86

Sado Island, known as a place of exile for religious and political leaders, is off Niigata on the Japan Sea and is Japan's fifth-largest island.

87

Suma beach is where the rival Minamoto and Taira clans fought in 1184.

92

All structures in Ise Shrine are made of plain cypress wood from the Kiso mountains.

99

Yoshino Hill, perhaps the most famous cherry-viewing spot in Japan, has four groves of around 100,000 trees, most of which are white mountain cherries.

115

In Japan, floors are covered with *tatami* (mats of woven straw), measuring six feet by three. The room Basho longs for is not much larger than a broom-closet.

116

Ueno and Asakusa, in Tokyo (old Edo), are famed for their temples (Ueno's Kan-eiji, Asakusa's Sensoji) and cherry trees.

122

Among the 'misted views' of Lake Omi (another name for Lake Biwa) is the 'Evening Bell at Miidera Temple'. The temple was founded in 674 in memory of Emperor Kobun, and at one time had 859 buildings within its great compound.

123

Benkei was Zen master to Lord Yoshitune of the Minamoto clan,
and helped him overcome his fear of death. Yoshitune, just before
going to battle against the Taira clan, appeared before Benkei
with sword upraised, demonstrating his new-found Zen daring.
The May carp, a kite symbolic of a boy's virility, is flown every-
where during the Boys' Festival, celebrated on 5 May, and for
some time after.

124

The cormorant is used by fishermen, especially on the Uji river: a
metal ring is placed around the bird's throat so that it cannot
swallow the fish it catches. Many tourists watch as the leashed
birds plunge for fish.

147

It is still customary to hire boats to view fireflies on lakes at
nightfall.

152

Left-over barley and rice are still the staple diet of Japanese dogs
and cats.

153

For another version of this poem, perhaps Basho's most famous,
see D. T. Suzuki's in the Introduction, p. 15.

156

In Basho's time, Hoshizaki Cape was a place known for its beauty.

157

From 794 to 1868 Japan's capital was Kyoto.

160

The time of the most active house-cleaning is just before the New
Year.

163
The Seta river, which flows from the south end of Lake Biwa, has a number of bridges, the best-known being Setahashi.

165
Known for its spectacular view, Mount Asama, near Yamada, has at its summit the Zen temple of Kongoshoji.

168
Crickets with distinctive chirps are prized as pets.

184
It is customary for travellers to pick up relics, often fans, at places they visit.

188
Matsushima (Pine-filled Island) is made up of more than 260 islands of various sizes and shapes in a great bay near Sendai. It is one of the 'Scenic Trio' of Japan, the other two being Amanohashidate on the Japan Sea and Itsukushima in Hiroshima Bay.

191
Pine-tree Law suggests the profound sense of the oneness of nature and religion.

198
A district of the Kiso river, with its well-known rapids.

205
This could be any one of the many large Buddha figures throughout the country.

210
Poem-cards are used in the ancient game of poem identification, played usually on holidays.

215

The poem relates to a famous passage in the book *Chuang Tzu* (translated by Arthur Waley): 'Once Chuang Tzu dreamt that he was a butterfly. He did not know that he had ever been anything but a butterfly and was content to hover from flower to flower. Suddenly he awoke and found to his astonishment that he was Chuang Tzu. But it was hard to be sure whether he really was Tzu and had only dreamt that he was a butterfly, or was really a butterfly, and was only dreaming that he was Tzu.'

217

The net of Law is the Buddhist *Dharma*, akin to natural laws.

235

The promontory, at Atsumi Peninsula's southern tip, is a scenic spot in one of the country's warmest districts.

237

Fukuura is a port of shelter on the Japan Sea in Yamagata Prefecture. Mount Atsumi, nearby, overlooks Atsumi Spa, a well-known tourist spot.

242

Chikusai was one of Basho's poet-heroes of the past.

247

At festival times cows (and oxen) were decorated to cart such things as fern and rice-cakes in processions. As in China, animals are associated with certain years in the zodiacal time system.

253

In a sense, requested as it was by disciples as he lay on his deathbed in Osaka, this is Basho's death poem. It is unquestionably the last poem he ever wrote.

THE STORY OF PENGUIN CLASSICS

Before 1946 ...'Classics' are mainly the domain of academics and students, without readable editions for everyone else. This all changes when a little-known classicist, E. V. Rieu, presents Penguin founder Allen Lane with the translation of Homer's *Odyssey* that he has been working on and reading to his wife Nelly in his spare time.

1946 *The Odyssey* becomes the first Penguin Classic published, and promptly sells three million copies. Suddenly, classic books are no longer for the privileged few.

1950s Rieu, now series editor, turns to professional writers for the best modern, readable translations, including Dorothy L. Sayers's *Inferno* and Robert Graves's *The Twelve Caesars*, which revives the salacious original.

1960s The Classics are given the distinctive black jackets that have remained a constant throughout the series's various looks. Rieu retires in 1964, hailing the Penguin Classics list as 'the greatest educative force of the 20th century'.

1970s A new generation of translators arrives to swell the Penguin Classics ranks, and the list grows to encompass more philosophy, religion, science, history and politics.

1980s The Penguin American Library joins the Classics stable, with titles such as *The Last of the Mohicans* safeguarded. Penguin Classics now offers the most comprehensive library of world literature available.

1990s The launch of Penguin Audiobooks brings the classics to a listening audience for the first time, and in 1999 the launch of the Penguin Classics website takes them online to a larger global readership than ever before.

The 21st Century Penguin Classics are rejacketed for the first time in nearly twenty years. This world famous series now consists of more than 1300 titles, making the widest range of the best books ever written available to millions – and constantly redefining the meaning of what makes a 'classic'.

The Odyssey continues ...

The best books ever written

PENGUIN CLASSICS

SINCE 1946

Find out more at www.penguinclassics.com